An Archæology of Revolution

MB Young

AN ARCHAEOLOGY OF REVOLUTION
Copyright © 2000 Marc B. Young

All rights reserved.

Cover photo by Stacey J. Young.

Back cover illustration by Julian Lorenzo.

ISBN 84-607-1335-0

Depósito legal: M-46.977-2000

Published by Calesius, CB
P.O. Box 1060
28080 Madrid, Spain

Printed by Campillo Nevado, S.A.
28019 Madrid, Spain

And spread out there it did, as it always had,

white fiery tips

drawing in the blue veil to itself,

glinting back its glimpses of the world but no single

slice distinct —

it would take them home, almost ten-thousand strong,

it hadn't moved

unstoppingly.

Home pulling easily

wherever they were,

unlike on groaning mountain ground where

passing friendly types

and angry types

checked one's hope at best, at best,

peninsula across for pay and grief

then north, not sure,

re-headed by a vote and aiming for the glistening back

no more, not sure.

Respiring gently in the pleasant light there it

was end all,

hardly hurried by the whoops of men —

yet the mass might now be cradled back.

Beneath the sea only the shaker could growl no.

—from Xenophon

An Archaeology of Revolution

I

Winter

    So inside his head
his matted head
  the one called Tratakeena
might have tried to sing the songs,
   ah vroom!
songs given by the folded one before and after blood was shed
beside the licking flames under a sheaf of rock
or with the oak tree's family
(to fly, to take off like the moon bird,
trail the soaring voice through blackened air
and sparkling give the night!)
   ah vroom!
But now they barely came to mind, the words,
frozen by the tension and the cold
so fend-off memories took their turn:
a morning's waking pink above the water snake
and stones to chase the gulls
   while the woman gathered things
— she whose face came out in sleep, or in the fire's flickering.
(Why do the trees take up the shrunken ones at last?
Would hands trace any other pictures on his back?)

    "Come on!
my feet are froze
your fight already done, come and get it now!"

Or thinking of another one whose mouth engulfed

while claws scraped long marks on his legs...

      ...when rumblings

from the dark realm of the spruce hit dusk cold clearing's air

ah vroom!

and smells announced a forager who once had naught to fear

      (and found the attitude persisting)

till time refined a spindly creature in whose hungry head

      great plots were hatched

so that the odds were close to even now.

But boldly went the pachyderm across the clearing for a drink,

its tentacle ignoring air,

contemptible of places where an ambush might be sprung

till sky was filled with peals that promised someone's death.

      And then

the blades pushed into shape so carefully drank blood,

ah vroom!

leapt and slashed through air to bury in thick hide,

and also tumble useless to the ground,

their wooden tails quick-snapped by whipping motions of a trunk,

so men (who come in groups but die alone)

      knew joy of wicked stabs and then a slip aside,

though two soon heard inside themselves the tune of crunching

      bones as well.

And Tra fought hard till they were three, just three,

and felt his fluted point glance off a tusk

An Archæology of Revolution

while staring in a gleaming reddened eye,
and breathing stinking wounded smells,
then backed away to help the battered ones
and let the cuts and cold invite inside
the huge-toothed mountain that they'd fought
the gloom that passes on some light.
Ah vroom!

*   *   *

The camp site cried:
"Oh, Drog!" Cheeks of leather teared,
a young face brown stroked red, the red of berries juicy tart
that crowd the branches in their gangs
and flowers dried, kept carefully, heaped upon his broken chest.
While another sat up breathing, heaving painfully,
the ribs collapsed;
his father own wore fields of years before dark death,
raven locks turned white, he had handfuls, less.

And overhead
in circle hung the hawk who'd let the comrades wing on south
when currents first turned cold, its mind
fixed on the birds that trees might jump or rabbits clearings cross
but brilliant eyes still gathering all,
from camp of men to tawny lion aimed in a fortuitous direction
to the brown-furred giant heaving flanks under a spruce
   beside the spring, afraid.

(The waves from where?

Fires of a childhood bursting in the black and white,

then days' slow calm,

the glens and hills where sustenance hangs down.

Now just a shrub, the little thing, grows huge,

it springs out at him!)

And down crashed

massive wobbly knees,

and crows and squirrels all heard the thud,

their caws and chatters sent the news, and bush-tailed dogs

arrived to hover in the trees,

await a chance at feasting less the fight.

But then fast back into the shadows drew these hungry youth when

currents of the air brought flavours of the spindlies,

beasts whose arms grow sharpened sticks

and mouths leave rarely scraps to eat.

(Oh all the summers

going carelessly, needles spreading soft under the trees,

the pleasant sun of morning light while steady,

quiet knocks the lake!

And then again the stab of pain,

the shiver starting ending in the head,

and big and small

and big and small, the dark the light and black again

and rising mountains beating back and forth.

And this too passed and ceded place to memories again.)

An Archæology of Revolution

      Then cracklings
of the bush there were and spindly legs hesitated too
then jerked back fast as huge cat's cough rang out,
         surprising from the bush.
And all the mastodont could do was stare through fever-boiling eyes
and leave his body open to a stab of any knife;
         then waves of madness faded with the light.
Ah vroom!

        *   *   *

      And snows
whipped deep one year
to hold them in between the squeezing rocks
while Tra saw in the sky a lake of white-flesh salmon leaping home,
leaping till their bodies filled his door.
      The folded one
his single eye turned back toward the stomach of the earth
spoke long with mothers, bears and corpless ones
who flitted down among the passages,
he said so as to know when snows would end
but surely more to pass the time.
Which played its lazy song,
while rocks in fatty hands became sharp graceful things
and boys piled sticks and turned bone hooks and
one chest broken by a blow was healed.

So under smelly rugs a woman moaned, a man who had or hadn't
fashioned all the shaft-heads he might need did too,
and children's stomachs roared till finally one morning's face
pushed through the landed bodies of the fish
that had turned snowy wall. Ah vroom!

                    Also a bear
fled stone showers
and strong-backed Tratakeena, on just a lark,
with fire on a stick
trailed their smooth cavern's throat into its sunless gut,
thinking there he might find things to tell
and learn from where the sound of endless dripping came.
Into a place whose walls and sky his torch revealed
were scraped in long-blade knives that
threatened to the tricky floor to pin his body, dead,
           while music of the pulsing liquid amplified;
so as his fire failed
back upward toward the world he ran,
the monsters nipping at his heels until the dancing lights.

Summer

        And snows
fled finally, unlike in tales of days when the world for reasons lost
had been enraged with men and beasts;
now yes,
       along the riverside the boldest flowers sprung
and humans clasped each others' hands
beside the colours of the warmth
accompanied by crows who saw it all, and told it all,
and sprites who gambolled in the branches
out of human sight and on the outcome
threw their polished bones and made their ribald jokes,
and passions everywhere had play,
       while waters free again rushed happy over rocks.

Melting, the black-maned family spread out on its shelf.

       For Tra,
nearing the morning of his daughter's birth and waiting for a sign
(with bulbous fruit's juice seeping to his head)
       the trees danced first,
the spruce with pine and oak and chestnut, finally the
       shrubs and boulders joining in
till after all the ground was stirred and plants exhausted,
bony fingers — sticks of dark brown wood —
signalled to the things to part.

Which they with loud groans did,
shuffling to the sides till bush-less lay wide plains
where Tra saw walking quietly a column of great beasts:
the rhino and the mastodont and giant bear
and lion of the curving teeth,
    the monster elk as well,
the young and old and fresh and feeble of their family,
while springs beneath two ancient eyes welled up, welled up.

    Like this passed quietly the falling day and all the night,
the column moving on invisibly under the black-blue sky —
but there for sure —
till finally, under the opening smile, just slow at first,
green bodies wound their way into another dance,
the spruce in sombre movement that perceptibly picked up
so others joined until an air of celebration reigned again;
even light-limbed babes from out the shadows of the boughs
    flew in and strong Tra too.
    And as he danced he knew the singing bears and wolves
and squirrels and flapping crows, their paws and bodies light
soft-brushing him from time to time,
sent words into his ear he couldn't understand
until at last he woke,
his back pressed on a needle bed, his head a knot —
its hardness having scooped in the soft ground a cavity —
    and trailing in his ears the fading
rhythms of the music from the earth.

An Archaeology of Revolution

      And in another
stretch of warmth, another turn, shafts flew and
bellies watered the soft ground in quarrels
till boiling rage gave up to compromise,
and other children came
and bones well-cleaned were found reposing in the woods;
they were the walked off ones
not taken by the sprites for games.
And days long whirled to change the faces of the family
until one soaking night of whipping winds
Tratakeena stretched out in his robes as well;
as the thing inside began to slip
his mind played with that drunken day, and thought about
the faces that he'd known, all those he knew.
      In any case
the children all can come back...

Ah vroom!

———————————

So then what got the digger on the road to everywhere,
inventing verse about long history?

Through weeks and months and more than a year
(but for times when thick-blown white weighed on their chests)
as all those generations green went dribbling through his hands
he'd searched,
until above, beside the germs of maple, hawthorn, plum and pine,
wedged loose in bed of spruce-filled peat
had been the mastodont, one tusk there, one gone.
        Christ how his heart had jumped
when that thing reached up from the ground!
Swallow it down, he did (the organ, not the beast)
while thoughts took on a hundred bulls misshapen,
moose and goat together in a joke,
a borrowed donkey killed, its compañero ox beside,
buried in a grave of tricks...
but sure, it was the mastodont.
And soon the fluted point of memory, not more,
tail and bite long crumbled in the earth.
Slasher of the beast? Could be. Though not its killer, possibly.

        Then down into the champagne days he'd gone,
as he would say,
each summer bone or tooth delirious gulp,
then hours resting full
while trees like barked arms pulled down suns;
        he thought he'd known the elephant's time!

No thought of ball, Ed Munch,
or smooth taut thigh-flesh in those tartan skirts,
and when he grabbed the weapon like a child he would conjure,
conjure up,
a human family to duck beneath a bough,
their faces now a million specks in thousands' years of dust
glowing only in a white imagination.

But then the echoed sounds came on,
grindings, groans evoking empty worlds and trunks,
the bursts of knowing-pleasure bearers of a gap
into which things fell, were lost, had missed
        and he would catch his mind adrift,
adrift,
staring at the monuments
or holding kitty's neck as if to look inside her green soup eyes.

So rattle through the entrails of this man! he thought at last,
about those sounds and groans,
sing struggles, woods and ships and matrons out of stone,
make those the frothy white and bubbling must sloshed on the earth —
        his offering, his sheep's life into flames.
What could be filler of the yawning space!

And a great distance later
        also not so far
in the land around the rivers that in places spread
then like the stroke of woman's hips to waist run closely
        in a curve
there was a celebration, there was a dance
for spongy land it had been drained.
        And singing mixed with the fermented drink
so woman rested chatted leaned on sacks set on the ground
and the children shrieked and played.
In the middle of a moment.
        Yet far from here
not so
by another river hunched some families
who took only what the wind decides, just what the wind decides
while watching for the gilled gods in the foam.
They were without a clue a moment now had come
defenders of a way

not suspecting the ascent.

An Archaeology of Revolution

Then

ting cling pop it's on,
in a leisure pocket of a day
by the counter topped above the trays of sea and earth,
a high wall's better part in mirrored glass.
Black drink tugged through foam of salt is the border of this place,
so flesh in wool and silk and cotton drops to rest.
And here the growling one who lost something
some time,
    a mother's age with progeny grown fat
and skin worked like a bomber coat
peddles sheets outside and wants another glass of fire juice
to smooth the morning joints.

    And there's a puzzling on the order of the things.
Then the digger — who's left his spade at home — is off.

An Archaeology of Revolution

II

So the three of us
(great friends since we were children grabbed across the sea
in what they call Illyricum)
Aemilio, Pivac, me,
we wasted little chance to run when Sulla's comrades turned
        toward the farm,
the sign the sky smoke-black above the Verus place;
Pivac the only one to turn his head,
        teaser of the Keepers underground.
Horses two of 'em we swiped
a chestnut stallion, night's own mare
who after dusk soft-faded from men's sight
and off toward the mountains raced to find
(somewhere after, near another sea more gentle tossed) the Rome.

        And all the world
was broken then, sad farms left to the shadows o' the trees and
Liber Pater, lost the hands of men
who'd jumped ahead of war, their sheep all dead
and corn stomped down, tails of cryin' in the air;
but three of us were helped out by the socii.
The spoils in their little way were ours.

Near the river after climbin' in the risin' land
we walked into a town a herdsman called Perusia,
place grown up in blue dawn's mist

its track connectin' all the stinks and human smells,

    the squawkin' coloured carts,

the food cooked up, the goats on rope,

the reek of waste and shit,

the eyes of men turned on my curves and tresses by.

The thick-doored wall ("shapes and lines

    of other men" — how'd Pivac know?)

we ducked to rest and eat on one horse sold,

and the boys, those two,

pretended to fill up the other tastes as well.

    Like:

        jugs poured full,

the crisp of kid and bread slow-dipped,

the slap and slide in rooms above,

while steady rapped the shutter wood.

    The shows they had in places!

Competitions of the strangest kind to do with mouths and orifices,

    women wound together in a pair,

old heads chantin' tales,

trials of different sorts

played to the songy voice of clink,

the curves and bulges of the wrastlers on the floor

and muscles, slap and sting —

while steady beat the shutter wood.

20

An Archæology of Revolution

      And there
in spots that we hung out met a beautiful man,
a bone-rack of a man
whose hair was white and fine, wore one eye pink
and smiled with gleamin' teeth and crimson gums
but who'd known cheeks turn into sacks
      weighed down as if by lifestones, heavy pits,
and waved dark purple stumps, two fingers on a hand, then
watched you at a half, his second eye spun darkly on the world.
And he stroked pictures of a land across the western sea
that almost washed on Rome,
today (he said) another pluckin' place of men.
"Mountains, hills and forests just like Italy
but also flats of rock scorched hot for miles
and earth a·sculpted brown and red
where you might wander till the dizziness and thirst slap you down flat
or cooling trees stand up beside their brook or spring
and gorge walls eagle 'round your head."

      And from his wine spurted up
the scenes that took their turns with teasin's of "his Livia":
"The Gracchus name's still whispered in the mouldy corners, streets.
'The destitute, the citizen, rebuild the world upon the farm!'
But words when are they dropped on cringing us?"
    Or so like that,
and the three of us knew nothin' of such headless things,
and thought our drinker strange enough
but took him on our way regardless.

        Then past more mountains
cool we went
and down into the lower lands of Italy,
livin' on the things we picked and killed and grabbed,
      we four,
Aemilio, Pivac, me, the man
trained in scrappin', horses, doin' clothes and
ships (he said he had done when on the coast),
roads (when not so near). Skills at chase: none.
But skies and air were bound up to our souls by thread:
we knew the signs of mood the day would show,
the sun at dawn and when it fell,
the colours passed, the lime of rain, the spots of worse,
the fluffs in afternoon on currents skin just feels.
To figure next day's progress or to know to
pass the hours whipped and damp under the spreadin' boughs
in talk, or in the rougher, softer games,
while our four bellies mourned aloud.

        We wouldda
gone right on to Rome but had a warning from some peddlin' men:
in the path an army growls, so swing away young things.
Then the old man asked: "Why not another pleasant place I know?
Some time we might get back to Rome."
      And so we turned toward the dark Campanian lands.

An Archæology of Revolution

        I want to say that
never would the town that spread under the green-furred rock
and milky boilin' sky have held us,
though months enough we passed there
trompin' laundry in the water and the piss,
        visitin' the houses too
here and there till that dark razor of the countryside whose friends
had freed us unintentionally all the way across the sleeve
set up siege at this place too.
(The word had been the Samnites and the others
were beginnin' to collapse.)
The truth: we were all used to city life and one of us
        (this pissed me so)
had dropped an eye upon a boy
who'd made a name inside the ring —
a corpse when later Pivac of all people found him anyway,
        the walls just down,
the blade's hilt oozin' in the stretch of his broad back.

        So squeezed in there we were,
the food and water scarce to the likes of us
        — though with my ways I scrounged up bits —
but soldiers took the town quite fast
and while they paid attention
to the Oscan-speaking types, some shabby 'Latin' youth
could soon enough slip off, melt in the crowd, prepare to go.

        Without the man, that is,
who claimed he had been everywhere,
and gave us as a gift a green stone polished bull, a small thing
that could hide inside a cloak or dangle from a neck
its tongue out-peekin' when it was shown off,
or, as the man would do, consulted on a comin' thing.
Now it was for us, to share.

        "And wound
a snake around us," said he as he'd presented it,
his odd eye dancin' wild, "so that there was no getting out for flies
and soldiers even dangled on the river
from the sky great daggered hands
and Scipio Aemilianus I would skin alive, the day I saw him
on some street where I have lived
but oh, Numantia, the shit is never there!"
        And like that he left us,
our companion in the ramblin' things,
three sides puzzled on the last day as the first
(though knowin' those words to the bull were some way tied).

        Then when the chance came up
we went to quit the villa where in all the chaos we had slept
(its owners run somewhere, their maze of rooms 'round sunny peristyle
in one o' which we sprawled, tense breathless in the heat,
my hands in hands of children also waitin' there)
while slidin' at our feet grew suddenly a battle scene,

An Archæology of Revolution

a wide-stone sea of chargin' mounts
some without their heads and legs and lords
so that when outside soldiers real started to make noise
we crouched and waited, eyes floor-stuck until they passed,
    and more.
    With darkness, finally, we quit the town.

    Across the water then,
ship-stowed amid a mass of crated animals
and amphorae of wine
with no idea of where we'd aimed,
while the earth it disappeared then stayed away for days,
popped up at last in islands ribbed in green
    and mountains pushin' high in the gods' home,
a second time by others painted grey against the sky
until two more sleeps ended in a dawn and a horned coastline
    in our hungry sight.

    And about my life
after the plunge into the brine desertin' all the geese and goats
to swim and smell the spray and listen for the jellyfish…?
Walkin', walkin' to a town Valentia, and then another called Saguntum.
    The narrow sweatin' coastal lands,
the blistered feet,
a sheep that Pivac killed, we had beside a path
and then the roofs of Centobriga.
In some days the work for those two on the road,
leavin' me the inn.

Land just like Italy but not,

the earth a bent and twisted red or brown

where you might wander till the dizziness and thirst knock you down flat

or trees rise up beside their brook or spring

       and gorge walls eagle 'round your head.

       And then the things

that might have thrown me to my fame,

or at least into a life well talked about, touchin' in a modest sense

two giant men I was almost with.

First:

The early soakin' mist when soldiers thought that chokin' life

       from our Aemilio,

burnin' holes and out an eye while underneath he squirmed and bit

could ease the dullness o' their day.

       Breathe. Just wait...

Second:

months, it was just months,

they worked the men throughout the night

until a tree broke Pivac's back as if he was a little stick.

       And then aloneliness, dead days of driftin' hours,

starin' at the green bull face as grief turned into heat.

Could be a tongue stuck out gave answers

when the gov'nor in what they called Hispania Citerior

rose up to break away —

I'd stuck a sword!
Our third edge could cut!

*   *   *

            Arevaci, Celtiberi
Vetones, Pelendones,
even Edetanos, Ilergetes some! With them
the chance to smash some heads and waste their blood
even if we fought along a Latin man;
Sertorius he made his promises, big promises.
    So first off to the south and west
where the earth was stone and red though also
ripplin' gold and olive in the fields
and there, between the Tagus and the Baetis warm
Caecilian Metellus saw his men go wailin' to the ground
while Mars's heavy hands drove through our backs encouragements
so that the groanin' fears that often swallow rage
let me go in time each time to shout and charge
and walk some more.
Others they were sure the yoke was off;
    "We're losing all the pus-face fuckers soon!"
    ⊔ Y/◇ ⋁ Q : ⁓
was painted by our writers on the captured chests
we left in places where they couldn't go unseen or read.

     And points of
hottest battles shifted north,
at the end of hikes over white-thick slopes with pine hills crouchin'
    by again.
Sybilian-whore they were an endless stream!
   In our noses armies fell,
bumblers ruined Roman plans again, again,
but later in the Ebro lowlands and the gaspin' mouth
we knew that we were thin,
began to feel as light as ghosts.
Pompey, pounded many times, came on;
    but this was all dragged over years.

    *   *   *

    Of course
you know the General (I mean Pompey)
in comin' back was not alone nor was he first.
On a merchant boat perhaps against the will of
several gods but with the pity of the owner of the ship I went
and rode with others through the storms and winds
that slugged us all around and back and forth
and added days if I recall that hadn't been there
when three youth first came to Iberia,
and all I hoped was if we crashed I'd, like that Greek,
live easy years upon an isle
but ah, some hands spread out the clouds to let in light
and our ship limped into a bay.

28

An Archæology of Revolution

    Though not a bay I knew,
nor one that struck a sound or smell
with others in the boat at first,
but the captain smiled at last and showed he sensed
where we'd found ground,
breathin' names I didn't know.

    And then began
the last part of these days,
on a land of mountains, groves,
and temples of the Greeks worn down,
goats and little boys with marks drawn on their cheeks,
fields that get a hundred things
then bake in flame-licked winds.
    Found a friendship with a man,
wandered down the coast with him and knew my hunger every day
until at last gave myself over at a farm where
I'd heard horses in the morn —
to find some calm was all I thought,
steer clear of death that in Iberia had gawked at me,
my thirst for blood filled up.

    And at the farm I worked, fed beasts and carried loads
as years before, and warmed a groom's bone limbs
    and let him do his things,
was surprised to find among the men

some rhythms of Iberia, and even sounds from further back,
somewhere, back of another sea...
    Anyway...
I cheered a few with words that still filled spots.
And for a time had a bit to eat and breathe.

But these were days when the world was squeezed,
no place escaped its goin's on, its drippin's and its stompin' down,
and words reached every ear,
so that one morning saw the family pack up the articles
that on a cart were luggable
and roll them off away,
while others jumped, their heartbeats in their mouths:
    not far away at all they said,
maybe 'tween the Charybdis and Scylla,
would come the pirate boats and a wave of men
pushin' at the world to turn it on its ear.
    To meet them, that'd be a thing.

So we went, on horses, group of us,
toward the point of land they'd said.
For me, though I was tired I was drawn so mightily,
mightily like when Aemilio turned his face toward the sky asleep,
to Pivac when the water shone his chest,
    to the early day when people feel they mustn't yell —
I was pulled along that way.

An Archaeology of Revolution

      And we came
ten of us to where the ones who'd know
confirmed was right and waited there, stared out to sea.
And there we waited stared and waited,
out to sea while it grew cold;
even the flakes o' sky came on our heads.
They'd said that here the one would come
to bring for all of us the breads and drinks
that put all hunger, thirst away for good
and so we waited patiently.
      Until that sky stayed dark
and waves whipped fierce and the monsters wailed;
and in the middle and the end came no good sign at all.

An Archaeology of Revolution

III

While for influence and leadership some prove themselves turning demons away.

So spent last night near the gorge
sipping ale and eating well,
resting, dreaming,
began meander up the path when the fireball
tipped past their heads,
a small sack on his back.
At the top where the watery roar was loudest
mist dampened face and
the wobbly throne straddled narrow crack
'cross rock.
"Will I do this?" thought brain that heights had always driven mad
chattering on the craggy testing ground
       designed by lords of the earth
dare not look, dare not look!
Thus when light was gone
he went astride the jiggly throne, seat of the test
and called to the breezes to chill his bones,
offered hymns to the trees
and the thrower who bursts the mistletoe,
stared straight ahead
tried not to shake his stony seat
while the demons came,
taunt and dance around his head

sought by their movements to

upset his balancing act.

But he stared through, sang praises to the ones

addressing oak that cloaked its noble self in night-time there.

    And verily verily black was long

longest of them all, but he went on

so that his song grew into crashing of the foam

and the breathing of the leaves

    and the blood-stunk face that danced in front

reeking of a battlefield strewn wide with brothers chopped

could not extract reply,

nor could the needly green that surrounded mother's face

bringing sweetest smells of arms and ground

sighing on about the pains he could be spared

if he'd plunge, plunge,

let down the burdens of ten years and two.

He was not favoured in any case,

cat's head mounted on the breasted trunk of woman hummed

    better let the arms of night caress,

take him to a padded bed.

But his hymns were the crashing falls

and the breathing of the trees

and he stared through jealous faces,

wobbled now and then.

Waited on the saving rays!

An Archæology of Revolution

And furthermore, furthermore it's said
that the crowds of Christians, such as they are,
were out to catch a man slipped free
a good deal short of forty-five odd years in jail
or whatever the sentence was.
Through a test of fire, Rev. Jim said he'd been.

Before the state clamped down on what were surely tricky books
three-quarters fraud you knew was floating in the air,
though not, some said, deserted by a glow of good.
Cherubic smile and warmth tamed one sceptic's hot abuse
       while
you'd need an oil rig to find the good inside the greasy rest of them
but Jimmy landed on the earth facing the wrong direction!
Can't bloody hearts be cleansed by that exploding rain
when off they dragged him for a half a century?
And then the lovely Tammy Faye, up and gone a sudden?

If you object that evil frauds should rot in jail until they die
the digger asks: what makes this brother so damn extra-bad?
In the end he admitted
that the condos and the Rolls were out of place.
While Tricky Dicky slaughtered tons and died a statesman,
his successors all drip blood. Do they apologize?
Compassion, not raison d'état, reigns 'round here.
So there!

Then the ball

on Johnny's foot,

he whacks it hard

to get it off

no matter if it goes the other way

       and all the mates shout:

"Why don't know pass your brother softly over here!"

Ignore them

till he's booted from the game

where he can think his way

and in the running crowd mostly avoid

the god-damn cowskin thing.

       To where?

The doorway of tomorrow

while the apple trees hang heavily.

How far to go with them?

Bob Cross who builds a barn in just a day

       won't answer when he's spoken to;

Jeremiah kicking harder than the rest

(balls as well as men)

an eye fixed on the lawyer's throat,

tallies better than the reeve

       but edges his plough off his strip

and sucks warm eggs he shouldn't have;

Reginald to mass but once tricked Stonewall's wife

with tales that humping might bring hip relief;

An Archaeology of Revolution

Gerald Brooke fined twice last year
for failing in his tasks —
poorly dug a ditch and never fixed the shed,
while Peter Vary's wife makes good ale
but gleaned twice when she shouldn't have
       and was found singing with that flautist in the tree.

    He tries
to wear down human foibles
so the builders of the Kingdom will fit in.
       The year is
      one thousand
      three hundred seventy-nine
      of our lord Jesus Christ.

       But shivering sweat, sweat
how many times since fires lit the way
and dirt got in our nails
has it been speculated on?
What lets us know
the reason next to everyone's long memory?
Better maybe:
       Angels do they sit on acorns when they chat with pigs?
Or everything, can't He be evil too,
exaggerate the price?

------------------------- Amen.

Remember though, don't take a world

spread with a shallow coat of dust

        where spindly feet

spring growths unheld.

But why, oh why as Father William asked,

did Jesus never spare a word for Spartacus?

Or did he know?

Or are we sure? Or are we sure.

And will I feel myself in their petty moments

        and the pounding of their feet?

        And now he's strayed too far,

the ball's on top of him again.

Don't whack it, bull it straight ahead

knocking over Joseph Mile

into his burly daughter too

which makes the cowskin squirt away —

        at least they think he's in the game,

don't shout at him:

"one too many balls are on the field!"

Then James ate Cross strips it

off young Mary Smith,

runs down the side to stuff it

in between the sticks

but Arthur thrusts a trunk in time in front.

James has also fallen in some shit.

        *   *   *

An Archæology of Revolution

Crackle swoosh crack
the fire different colours
smoky afternoon
creak of wagons bringing men;
he rubs his dirty whiskered face
        and wonders what he's done.
"Velvet camlet lined with squirrel and ermine"
not for us
colder wetter things
but they seem easier to bear
        quite suddenly
since still the carefree spaces come
sunlight splashing down a hill
        a thousand children in their bloom
and sips and bites on Sunday afternoon;
...The crackles different colours under smoke
the squeal of wagons bringing men
....No,
        the priest John Ball knew himself
in the pounding of their feet.

The year: a thousand
        three-hundred eighty-one
        of our Lord Jesus Christ.

Then riding south the cables of the Church back home to Italy

it's a winter's soaking night;

His Holiness Leo X wraps himself in coats and slippers

'round thick socks

to creep downstairs,

look carefully at death spread in its mother's arms.

    Marble of the skin, the skin of marble

all must see

plop plop plop there is a drip somewhere and

Leo lifts his light up high and squeezes close his nose

as if to sniff the sooth that grieves

but oh! Marble of the skin, the skin of marble

    reassures him, makes him worry

ribbed and muscled one spread naked in those whitest arms...

till nothing's there outside dripping experience

and the gnashing of the one

who couldn't snatch her own from the snarls of the day

    and knows that's how it ends.

She holds him, wom-girl, holds up the wasted one, limb sent gently

underneath his own with strength beyond the bits of rancour spent

while Leo sticks his nose as close as possible

to gaze into the face that's tilted back and thinks:

    we're all just going on about our things,

better in a sense like this, revealed.

But the Florentine would count the inches that remain

for all the coloured velvet tales wound up in layers thick on top,

the ones he uses as his seat and vantage point,
their garment days all done.
      Damn dead lambs and pretty ewes! he almost says aloud.
Is that a shearing sound as well?
Oh, shiver shiver twitch he would,
the sin will stick around and plop!
the rain is dripping in.

So sob you others too beside this gleaming end
as dead months ride away.

Then back a bit, up to Sandro Botti.'s town,
colours in the place of flesh and stone.

And when he'd drunk from pages all he'd need,
Left the workshop of Filippo Lippi,
Stroked with graceful lines his early deeds,
Muse brought the fragrant droplets from the sea
To let him know with whiff of pungent life
The rose petals' cascade midst god's white milk
Light zephyr-driven as the hour was midwife,
Soft-wrapped in flowered robe of wind-wound silk
Along a sandy line of Cyprus coast
Where her straw hair says love is pale and chaste
And green-sun waters are the mother host —
No grinning bellies sink into the base.
But flawless beauty too will cede the day,
Then tense in prayer he can while away.

Like all o' them who take it heavily.

An Archæology of Revolution

Last,

beg those sunken eyes,

try again old starry flow,

see if in the jumping of the toad,

the baby llama's gait, there is a hint for Tahuantinsuyu...

    but bodies move as they would

        while bodies under scream and fester, choke, expire.

Not since from out the cold folds of the lake

light took toward the sky

and siblings hardened into stone

has there passed this

    but bodies move as they would

        while bodies under scream their agony and fester,

choke and stink;

and who knows, who knows, think eyes:

the giants had their day in Tiwanaku, then were done —

could be another grand inversion's underway.

If we could only see.

The world's in four,

the fox leaps in his place

but bodies scream and stink and burst.

    Might be the ground is sucking in the sky;

if we could only see.

IV

But now it's time to get up off your ass and make a buck.

It wasn't that I knew the Vizier himself
(though true, I'd been presented once
peddler of some glassware, figurines from Delft)
but that I'd lived in Istanbul — five years, seven months.

So I knew the Turkish skills and arts,
one in particular that later brought me some success
though in that deal I might have shunned a part
had I known the wage exacted in duress.

For you've heard sometime in '82
long after with our blond-haired swarthy progeny
we'd settled on the cool Danube
K. Mustafa took it in his head to spread the Turks' hegemony.

To enhance his rule he thought he'd lead Vienna's sack
and with 200,000 warriors quit the frontiers of the Ottoman —
adieu to Sultan Mehmet who'd play upon his back —
to aim the crippling blow at Christendom.

By then I was with the Duke of Lorraine
who ran the army of the Austrias in those trying days
and we rode out to slow the surging tide of men
before around the walls their crescent arm arrayed.

I 'volunteered' to duck back into town as the siege was almost set,
thinking my accented wife could meet some nasty turn
and wanting to curtail this most immediate threat;
she'd be tempting if her countrymen were leisurely to burn.

The Turks soon offered their terms for surrender,
said if the gates were opened streets would not run red
but all perfidies real *and* never done can be remembered;
Mahound had made no reputation tucking small Serbs into bed.

Indeed 'twas said that at a spot along the way
the Vizier'd requested one unblemished flaxen messenger
to bear a quivering town's communiqué;
no harm of course would fall on her.

Then in a ceremony with a sharpened blade
he'd lopped her bawling head onto the grass,
mounted it upon a pole and sent it on parade —
convincing all besieged to block his boiling mass.

But hardly did the Turks rush fierce upon Vienna's walls
but as I feared employed the starving tack instead
mixed in with missile sauce at intervals,
leaving us to wrestle with our dread.

An Archaeology of Revolution

At last I said I'd bear a message to Lorraine,
slip through the half-moon camp pretending I was Turk,
after a swim report the Viennese were rotting in their den;
if help long tarried it wouldn't have much work.

But soon oh holy Mary! Saxons, Poles crashed through the trees!
the wooded hills toward the north
forcing heathen's body first to rise, then flee,
letting our bedraggled from out the gates surge forth!

And now comes the commercial theme —
for the Turks abandoned treasures dragged through Hungary,
among them one small tent piled high with sacks of beans
which to my travelled eyes were no mere curiosity.

Thus while the noble allies bickered over jewellery, rugs and gold
(lovely things — in this the infidel renowned),
I wondered if a hot black drink could be Vienna sold
as in the kahveh houses of a Muslim town.

Within some months I'd set up shop with my one partner —
a chap at watch for schemes of interest —
to wrestle with our brew, add sugar, cream as lightener,
roast the fruit a little longer, less.

Until at last a number tolerable of the Viennese
were willing to imbibe it with their afternoon thick tortes
and one day dearest Leopold served a pot after the cheese
(though to be sure the dinner guests were Magyar lords).

My sons were never sure there was a future in kahveh,
above all when the beans ran out
and I'd lead yet another buying trip away.
I don't know if they ever downed their doubt.

An Archaeology of Revolution

Now the Dutchie Anton de Kuyper, what did he do?
    Just had a hand in the new sensibility that understood
how metal's jingle is the clearest tune
and that you play it buying cheap from Heinz
and selling dear to Julian, respecting, really, nothing else
fighting only when you absolutely must
since commerce doesn't like that every Thursday's interrupted
    by a siege.
        Hence a family
almost entirely from peaceful intercourse
was made (as we like to say)
though an uncle did accompany the Admiral Piet Heyn when 1628
saw the silver fleet of Mexico fall into clean
Dutch reformed hands
and holdings in the West Indies Company
paid dividends of over seventy per cent;
but man, every story has its turns...

    So
        one time or other
they brought marble on from Italy
    timber from the Baltic states
(cousins drained the marshes of the Tuscany)
sugar, smoking stuff across the sea
    wine for a time from Portugal
had a go with Australian aboriginals
but found the trip too long to bring back many still alive
at the second ocean's end

and even for a laugh if it wasn't for the clink
helped furnish ships for one side in a Scandinavian war
(1645)
while family friends from Rotterdam built the vessels of the enemy.
Just God blow it from the Zuiderzee!

        And early in a
second generation's fabulous success
(speaking here of Anton the eldest shortly after turning forty-six)
into the corporation of the greatest city in the world they went
— the town council, that is —
warehouse, workshop, bank to smooth
the pull allowing better things to be enjoyed.
A regent family in Amsterdam
        city of a state
where the cities ruled the roost
and the centre couldn't do a thing... unless

        So gradually Anton left the running of the fleet
to others in the family
gave himself primarily to wise administration
took on the key tasks of the time.
        Which were:
Keep the peace so that the lanes stay open
(even if at times one has to back down to the Roi
and soft-brained Hapsburgs here and there);
Keep the predikants in check
who preach a Godly place where pages sizzle, smoke

An Archæology of Revolution

Catholics who run good businesses get turfed;
Keep the grauw, the rabble in its place
for really only those whose minds are free from other cares
are fit to nudge the state.
Those the key tasks of the time.

A free state, not too free but more than any other found in Europe
where you say and read just what you like
(in Dutch and French primarily)
pray to God in your accustomed style
       live without the leeches and the landed types
who take take take
build their glory grabbing other lands
sow ignorance and want
impose some creature in a funny hat
No.
       A new state, an old state, a perfect state
Anton thought they'd made in the United Netherlands —
screw those kingly fashions of the day.

       *   *   *

       He liked his wine in cups,
was known to keep two going at the time,
enjoyed a pint of dark brewed ale at lunch
and when the city's business in the afternoon was done;
took his cheeses, ham for breakfast sliced on thick black bread,
favoured most of all a pheasant in an orange sauce

and smooth dark ruby fortified, after the piece of fruit.

    Adored the winter country walks,

the dogs run fast ahead burst ground birds in the cold.

Learned, a little painfully, to play the cello,

    even wrote a piece

then for all intents and purposes gave up on that

but like so many Dutchmen didn't have to feign his love for paints;

could be that ochres bubbled from the ground

    right into veins at birth.

    Had his portrait done of course,

    collected history pieces,

finer works in his view than the preachy boards:

no Van Ostades on his wall

nor Dou

nor Steen

(he'd eat oysters when he felt like it,

indulge the appetites they grew).

But Rembrandt, there that one was a veritable regent of the brush

and when in 1662 the corporation and the citizens found fault

with one-eyed glowing Claudius Civilis

    (panel 'round the new town hall

    back to AD 69)

Anton, a man of taste, he disagreed,

knowing when bright oils breathe some glory

and should be kept in place.

For neither a fanatic nor a parvenu

    nor a swiller from the docks was he.

An Archæology of Revolution

      Things only hit a snag 'round 1670 when the peaceful
peddling-at-all-costs group under Councillor de Witt
brought the country into wealthy envied isolation
just as Louis planned a push into the Dutch Republic's heart.
      Here it must be said the Kuypers bore some blame,
a little blame
for one nephew had invested heavily
as part of the monopoly on wine along the River Loire,
even kept a splendid house at Nantes
and for a bit before French armies swarmed up north
had argued hard for time more time, that pacifying time
      since battling the French would be a bad idea —
war you know aristocratic sport and game and waste of time.
      Steady though
in Paris there'd been Colbert building up the industry and trade
inviting Dutchmen, Germans in to teach the weaving, mining arts
so that the realm could buy huge armies, fund campaigns
      and squeeze the Netherlands into a sack.

      In any case
after the Frenchies pushed and the people rose
to throw aside the Stadholderless regime
      in favour of the Prince of Orange
and
Johan de Witt, his brother too, were slaughtered by the mob
      outside the jail,

after all of that,
the Kuyper lad who'd floated wine along the Loire
plus Anton too
spent a little time locked up, though just a little time
until the Orange William put things
pretty much the way they'd been before.

Except that '74 — when the French got out — saw isolation end
as soon would go the high times in the Netherlands
forged when ease and money
hadn't made the traders and the nudgers fat.

V

Then in a sudden twist his cousin Chad announced
he would vacation a mite differently this year,
not far from Spanish surf but with a little culture too —
the accounts had come of late in droves,
now to push horizons back.
A fuller person's on the Chadder's mind.

              *   *   *

Set up in the line, then, cousin, digger and a friend,
a longish line (that snakes around the lot,
cooks the tourists pink)
chattin' Philadelphia
while breathing Andalus perfume
and thinking on the loops of gold
that melt your gaze into a wall of sandy, sandy tongue.

    "The beauty wails enough
but I'll feel lost inside the shell:
foreign jewels and spirit stand remote
to my Western kind of eye."

    Still, shit,
as one old man said from a stage,
got to shake out all the epochs for their worth;
this time with this one

perhaps alleviate the crisis racking young America.
    Fast then,
before they even get in through the gate,
drop their chat,
round up one young Rafael,
Christian gentleman from a good family
    born 1025 in Cordoba
(415 on our Muslim Brothers' count)
which say the chroniclers
was one bright shining centre
where the groups together did all right;
"We'll wring some counsel out of him."
The press on certain themes begins.

    Fluent in Romance is Rafael, though he
prefers it all in Arabic
(browning off the smelly priests)
but when they want to keep the press
this Rafael begins reciting things:

My eyes drink first sip of her in the shading of the dusk
Beneath the lemon tree she flees the glance of lust...

Cut right off that rhyming scheme.
    So does he hang with some who bow to Mecca when they pray?
Of course.
Though Berbers... doesn't really like.

And are the Christians left alone
to keep their Sabbath, eat their pigs,
imbibe from fancy metal cups?
Of course.

And yes one drifts toward the mosque,
apex of brilliance all around
(they move up to the gate)
while the Catholic realms up north grind on without –
    Rafael he's been around, he knows.

My eyes drink first sip of her in the shading of the dusk
Beneath the lemon tree she flees the glance of lust...

Examples they demand, seen so far
no more than shell.

    Heavy ships
weighed down with grain and luxury;
    the art of war done perfectly
(though cities spinning their own way,
northern Christians starting hard to press);
sculpted words;
seas of coloured patterns to infinity;
gardens singing in the summer heat;
the astrolabe caught movements,
fine silks spun from out of worms.
    "You know in Cordoba in 1013

was published
by the pen of Abu-l-Qasim Jalaf al-Zahrawí
a medical encyclopaedia from Dioscorides the Greek
while Ibn Zaydun sung his verse
and Ibn Hazim spoke of love,
we know of love in the garden of Al-Andalus."

My eyes drink first sip of her in the shading of the dusk
Beneath the lemon tree she flees the glance of lust.

Then through the weeks I wait around the marketplace
Hanging by the fruit and spice for that smooth kohl-dark face
Jumping, starting, feeling passion rise so many times... alas, no trace;
It seems that never will she come, but see her brown full curves I must
Until at last through trees she glides, that tender mouth...
Bud pink and less a trace of trust.

Later in the cinnamon breeze in respite from the hot love of the sun
We lie together shyly, one eye tracing shoulder bare under a shawl
    undone
Hand toward the gentle heaving of her breast, doubting now that
    she will run.
Mouth with the other eye shares thoughts about the roundness of a bust
While nose out-stretches to inhale her musk.
But no, she pushes fruit between my lips, pulls away when they
    continue for a kiss
As antelope when nearly taken by the cheetah slips to make the
    charge a miss

And holds her finger in my face, putting off our sweet-mad bliss;
The moon is witness to the barrier she raises to my thrust.
I'll have to writhe, make promises — no love will flow from actions brusque.

But at last she speaks: "If you touched me I'd burn you like a crust
Then on this soft-grassed ground your flesh would turn to dust."

When he seems done
they ask about Averroes (?)
(friend from Philly thinks he's called),
man who was for justice,
said the universe leans down for probing minds,
but Rafael was done
before the master was a babe
(dates had better keep them straight)
so put it to him
why his family would go to church
considering the fashions of the day.

"We were an old Hispano-Roman clan...
My father claimed
that while elites of Visigoth
gave up the Church too painlessly,
turned by their ne'er forgotten Arian heresy,
we were saved
by our strong Latin faith in God cum man

that made the difference clear enough
(without especial fuss)
    while mother thanked a statue kept
through generations of her line,
a painted woman on a chair —
she was about knee-high — a copy of a cemetery piece
we said lived farther west and south.
The holy Mother of the Earth,
heathenish in Muslim eyes, an 'anchor for our Christian ship,'
as my own always says.

    "My theory was
we wanted family interests to remain in vines;
Islamicized that might have been a trick,
precisely since we liked to taste.

    "As to your thing,
we kept it going more or less because
in the tension lines were drawn
and there were held... certain priorities."

But at last she speaks: "If you touched me I'd burn you like a crust
Then on this soft-grassed ground your flesh would turn to dust."

An Archaeology of Revolution

VI

Maggie (to the New World):

An emerald spring
a million painted faces open
days enough of sky blue sky
then it's the last (and I see crystal on the pink wet skin).

                                    We go up and down
                                            and up
                          my stomach jumps toward my throat
                          and leaves a part with foamy Neptune.
                This is a breathing heaving beast, and we're a mouse
                                    upon its chest!

Summer's devils
in the night around one's neck
feet white empty of all sense.
The pulling, grinding of the days
the body cries for rest at thirty-one.
But oh, the babies are so beautiful!

                            Lights dance goblins all around
                                a wave of foreheads, eyes
                              incandescent, incandescent
                                    no noise, no pain
                            only a mouth's long sighing shape.
                      I'll see you all again, my precious things!

                                        END STEP ONE.

VII

Stop now, you, right here, says the digger-poet to himself.
At this point what's got to be put down
is a certain impatience, like:
    we've inspected all the bushes,
smelled some pretty flowers one by one,
time to pack the rest up in a bunch
    and go,
tu sais?
Jump
    squeeze, compress, fold, it could be done,
*time is run*ning out in any case, an urgency an urgency
    or
the 1789 solution and start that calendar again from scratch
today, right here, from the sunny church above the Place Mayor,
Chinchon
where José Antonio Pri o de Ri e   is still etched
(but for his letters that ain't)
    and the Brits wear shorts
while Clinton prefers Olivo to the Polo della Libertà in Rome
(imagine that: the types who spent their lives
    rolling spaghetti communism
now favoured in the mosquito swamp).
Pourquois ris-tu sous cape, jeune homme?
Noah tired halfway through the ark,
no doubt some favoured leaving shorter that stone snake
that bellies through the Chinese countryside,

especially the ones who lugged the stuff.

    Uncle Joe was tempted too,

collectivize the half and call it done.

Aunt Beulah later said a little pregnant was better than a lot,

though she wasn't prone to nausea.

    It's just that there's an urge to get it done.

But resist a bit,

    resist.

    We gathered in the early morning in a pub way up on Yonge,

    checked the guns, all had a shot,

heard the Lyon talk

then marched to meet the redcoats in a field.

    Didn't go as well as underneath the wood and watered line,

got no darn republic at the other end,

what's worse we were defamed by blue-ass historians

who said we took off at a burst

as if their fat side ever left a seat...

Stop that

    stop

...He took a room in a pueblo inside Aragón

paid three days

stood out in the early morning with the olive trees
> in contemplation of his death
> in contemplation of his afternoon
and walked around the old men on their chairs...

...While on their earth other ones snoozed
earth cut in shelves that steam
the shadows of their mothers in the air;
they'd rubbed well the old earth's skin and
scratched away the itch
then taken gifts of favour as they rose.
> Right here men came to rip their walls at night
their own men near, almost their own
a moment and a thousand bleeding swipes.
Hyena's cackle as the moon lights shapes away —
what plague of madness this?
The blades intended for the sun-drenched stalk
stroke belly of a child
not even one cry can be heard
> so bludgeoned by the chorus.
They're like the herd that must be penned and killed
for reasons it will never get
> and there's no more...
no more....

...And she hadn't done a thing

thud thud

        just came home to find him loaded, cocked

too much power of the wrong kind

not enough the right

        steeped together in a keg

smacked her till her cheeks and eyes were purple, blue and red

tricolore of the Kingdom of the Gradual Death

        smash

        smash

        ahgh!

        shit

        whore you whore you know I'll smack ya good!

You always ask me that! Why can't you let me fucking be!

Throbbing rainbow of a face she should have known before.

zzzzzzzzzzzzzzzzzzzzzzzzzzzzzzzz, f..k zzzzzzzzzzzzzzzz

        Then

a corner jabs into her back

        the floor she knows tis hard

she knows

remembers how it grinds her points like stone...

But back to greater themes...

Goering, that bloated make-up-caked drug addict of a thief
    lost weight on prison food was weaned off pills and cream
        regained his pluck refused to whine
            fought back spoke well acted like a man.
                Though confirmed as Satan
                      held out for a marble
                          sarcophagus.

While Jodl spoke his back erect he was loved by his wife
    Kaltenbrunner lied lied lied lied crowed he was defamed
        Ribbentrop droned sheaves of blood diplomacy
            Sauckel didn't put the maggots in the food
                Schirach faced up to the crimes
                    Rosenberg could not be
                      Understood.

Justice might have been served by an ID bullet in the head
    but this a grisly processing of death orchestrated
        (less Herr Strauss) under the rules of defence
            letting the intellectuals off the hook.
                After a trial don't use the noose
                    even if some scoundrels go
                        with dignity.

Then stick to something now. Don't jump around so much.
But some false dividers are gonna melt away.

           *   *   *

Now Arnaud is on the run in early summer, '89,
      where he's running is through the centre of les Tuileries
to grab a bridge and get across, maybe take la rue de Seine
but the perfumes cling to him
      the honey smells are shrouds;
perhaps they're from the petalled pregnant air, the sunlit sticky air,
but Arnaud he thinks, no, knows
they still waft up from in between those great white breasts
that had filled up his mouth
(though never quite enough)
and trembling breathing harder parts that slid his pushing hands
      lorsqu'il a été frappé par cette tarte aux poires et flan
that he was supposed to make today, that pie of pear.
      L'abbé l'avait demandé, le pauvre Arnaud l'avait oublié
when in the middle of a splendid silken thrust
a fleshy perfume drop,
maybe the tail end of a gasp
      or the squeezing of that perfect fit somehow
had brought it back to him, painted pie inside his head
— now's the time to run.
The palace of the abbot where he baked, run, run,
away from the service at the sucking hills...

An Archaeology of Revolution

And on the quai he went against the current of an angry band
bound for what will be one day the place de la Concorde,
declined all calls to come along —
in all the humping he'd forgotten sweet fruit pie
>and had to run.
>Indeed, the pâte sucrée was done,
but the pears they hadn't even had their scalding bath.

But ah, pause, stop again, o' course...!

VIII

Ho! Then how to begin an importantisima thing
        almost forgotten
(tu dormais, toi);
might be you have to hop around to different places very fast
        or worse
get your tinder up at once
inside the zillion stony circles of the world.
Scratch that —
        Korean just ain't Szechuan,
Memphis can barbeque all night and Kansas fry its chickens in a pan
        batterless,
Venezia's still a farther run than an ocean and a boot,
a pond before some squishy turf;
        so pick your spots.

To one we haven't been before,
        behind our longest reach:
a family at early Cantonese,
they're following the blackened path
where fire whipped through trees and roasted dry a field
and caught some residents as well;
one fat oinker panicked, dashed another way
into the poison breaths of fiery death
and he's found by our experimental family —
tasting even better now.
Though 'cause the looing sauce hasn't shown up yet

we could be anywhere in any mobile kitchen/abattoir
on God's green-yellow earth.

Change of scene.
        This one we've cut close to, spatially at least.
Between the seven hills (that's Rome)
shortly after she-wolf gave boys suck
(you know a statue of this crouches by Segovia's aqueduct
where in the future far they'll prepare stupendous baby pig),
grains are pestle-pounded, pestle-ground,
mixed with milk and water-cooked into a mush —
and this is what our brothers eat.
Or chestnut meal polenta cakes.
        But don't lament,
the line that stretches to the waist of Julia's
already being drawn not far from here, not far away at all;
in the sea-thrust lands where Zeus looks down
they've made important gains.

        E.g. some say
the chef named Orion's already heated a full bowl of milk
        until it froths,
envelopes in its waves wheat flour browned in oil, gently
bubbled till it's thick
to dress the heads of vegetables,
a rabbit baked inside a pot, while...
        and though Vergilius Maro did the poem
dónde estaríamos sin las hermanas negras, verdes, tintos

An Archaeology of Revolution

of our scraped ground
       our thirsty pregnant ground,
no juice to blur the cares or golden lubricant etc., etc...?
Though as we said it's done.

       And the gratiné is on its way,
cheese and crumbs climbing the necks of artichokes and leeks.
(Avgolemono lemon silk: not ready yet,
Europe has to wait for seeds of trees from Palestine;
and neither has smooth yogurt swallowed garlic shown,
still pending is that dairy wisdom from some Bulgar friends.)
Tender points asparagus
breads of seeds and spices, flowers, wine
washed down by yellow Spartan sun and the juices of the pine
when Grecian heat cuts honeyed air.
       Also, also, the eggs have broken in the pan.
       Most of this will be carted to the seven hills
when those hills cross another sea.

But before we're carried off into the kitchen
sequestered by the Tuscans and the Gauls
pay the dues eater, pay the dues
for toward the rising face
they've moved far past the piggy finished in the flames.
The kitchen of the kitchens,
and never mind provincial boasters here and there.
       So sit ya down to lunch.

A spot.

      Robert Aubry relaxes in the timid castings of the lamp,
a flute soft warbles from an antechamber,
the men around him are all old
      Chen Tian

      Ming Xiu

      Tin Li

      Siu Chong Ng

      Tin Fei

They are all old, each of them
      taking up the same spot at the table round.
While in a rush to senses, each forgetting what the other is,
      the waves of warbling flute mix up
with smells, such moaning smells
so that the ears and nose fight hard to sort and separate the gifts
that rightfully accrue to each.
And Robert — not the old men in their chairs — wriggles urgently,
      impatiently.

      Begins.

      Bowls of bright flame vegetables
green string beans, carrots broccoli
      bell peppers red
they're cold and pickled when young Robert bites
though they pause at table only seconds on their way;
the old men look and murmur, don't touch just smile a bit
      and look and murmur, smile a bit

(someone didn't teach the young white devil everything).
Cold chicken sesame dressed in lettuce on a plate
    walnuts browned and sweet
(Tin Fei he stirs himself to pluck a nut)
    dumplings by the dish
Ha Gow
Shu-Mei
small eggs — must be the children of a smaller bird riding on the heads
of meat —
    they all pause only seconds on their way
back from whence they came
and the old men look and murmur, smile a bit
(someone didn't teach the young white devil everything)
    just look and murmur, smile a bit
while R. Aubry grabs for what he can in the seconds that are there.
It is delicious, he is famished — just one thing...
but perhaps the old men in their leather age have lost their appetites.

    And then a snaky thing in sections comes along
bathing in a mud dark sauce.
Hah! All of the old men sample this
(Robert he still eats more).
    Bowls of eggplant, pork, together under sprouts of green
the snow-white grains of water lands
they're nibbling now
    Chen Tian
    Ming Xiu
    Tin Li

        Siu Chong Ng
        Tin Fei
beginning to yap louder too.
Robert of course can't follow all this chat,
though certain things are sure,
one of them that his stomach doesn't stretch much more,
could be they're saying that
        (his Cantonese is slow).
Chestnuts with green beans
chestnuts chicken
chicken wearing belt of leek
        a steamed fish covered in black beans
a bit more of the snow-grain scooped into the mouth
        (someone didn't teach the young white devil everything)
and then a bowl, huge bowl
which at the table takes a pool of clear rice wine
into which are plunked to swim the shrimp
        live shrimp
that soon begin to leap and bang themselves
into the clear glass of the lid
(they are as Robert Aubry was one night,
their lid the hanging ceiling of the lodgings of his friend,
but unlike him they leave to bathe in a hot wash of chicken broth)
        and here the men eat too
        jawing wildly all the while
moving next to sweet prawns butterflied, asparagus just cooled
(Robert no longer bears the sights)
        and scallops tossed in snapping sauce and celery

An Archæology of Revolution

    fried milk with crab.
The spirit of a stomach stumbles to the singing flute
    (they didn't teach the young man everything).
The guest will miss the soup, it seems.

    Another spot.

The train has carried him to the Auvergne
    into the burst of reddish-orange roofs
among the mountains worn like soaps swum too long in the tub.
That evening out from the hotel in streets that climb cathedral hill
    vers le village de Chamalières
        où cet homme a veçu, il y a longtemps,
loué une chambre, une cuisine,
aimait une fille (quand ils ne hurlaient pas à cause de n' importe quoi).
Where he loved that girl when they weren't howling over
    who knows what.
Now he's been deposited right back, in part, to eat.

An alley called if it wasn't too a street
    there's the July heat
the cinés tucked away that don't show Costner, Depardieu
and the women waiting for the dusk
    beside, beside a dining room
(they're cats, though leather boots ride up their thighs,
their brown and golden hair take droplets from the light).

He feels quite timid, hungry, warm
        walks past a woman
hangs outside the doorway pausing with the trepidation
that will never leave him all alone
then steps into a pleasant dining room
empty — he hopes — of the world.

        Remember, our man is here to eat,
in part at least.
Omble chevalier (that's char, he had to search the memory for that)
with asparagus and truffles black,
the spread of liver cream from bursting organ of a goose,
        a bit,
some lamb kidneys dressed up in Roquefort
then the baby's rest rubbed rosemary
and carrots honeyed, garlic mashed into a mound of white
with gentle crust of cheese.
And with the fragrant child of sheep arrives a woman from outside,
takes a table near the back
she and the owner chat
she has a bottle of champagne
she is quite beautiful, hard legs, full breasts, hair black.
        The eater's also doing well with his red bottle
and the local Saint Nectaire
and he's relaxed.
        He's sipping coffee when she looks around.

A final stop.

>Don't stray too far from the appointed places,

touch some ground under the fecund skies

where de Kuyper might have been.

>It's the war, though the bombs have stopped

after five stretched days

(the place ain't got the mettle that it used to have)

and fighting's not the only thing slowed down

but eating too (according to a woman who lived through the thing).

The young men sent off to the factories in Hitlerland,

the produce of the farm going three potential ways:

>>the German army, consumer of the best stuff,

cheeses and the porkers too;

Second, the German population (no prizes there but what you

>>could call edible);

Third, the Dutchies needed for the sweeping up and tightening of

the bolts, for them some fragrant scrunge.

>So what exactly's been the tumble in the eating standard?

e.g.

>family of a bakery hand

they ate potatoes — in the past — and a vegetable each night

(boiled, naturally), gravy of a sort our survivor says.

An Orange once a year (at Christmas time)

and every Sunday one small piece of meat for everyone.

>Full stop.

> Apparently when school was done

the children used to put potatoes in the ashes of the stove

and have them baked,

> that was the snack.

> Full stop.

Now with the war, as it winds up and down

> (the Krauts cut off in Stalingrad,

tensed feet touched rocks washed smooth off Normandy),

all the treats above are gone

> replaced by a soup-kitchen not so aptly named

since the stuff they dish is water with a vegetable warmed up,

not near the liquid luxury our early Cantonese enjoyed —

bones boiled in the stomach of a dog.

> No, this is water with a vegetable

warmed up, taken in the water kitchen

communal dining Nat. Soc. style,

this paucity of gourmandise

going on until the Cross throws packages from planes

of sausage, chocolate, bread.

> Manna

white as snow and soft as angel cake our survivor says

which some people, their stomachs shrivelled from a year of 'soup'

gorge on till they die.

> Imagine that.

Their human lives run out and turned to something else,

so they are killed by human food.

> Like cats fed onion pie.

An Archaeology of Revolution

VII (*a little more*)

Now back to Arnaud scurrying along, he hasn't made it yet,
he's staring at the rue Jacob
and what has to be absolutely clear
    there can be no mistake,
is that he's forgotten the gang of angry men he passed,
knows only dimly, very dimly
that in May of the year past the parlements were stripped of weight,
has no idea Necker restored their rights,
frankly hasn't thought if the Estates should count their heads together
    or in the separate groups.
Thinks mainly of his pleasures and his work, like that,
but
    but:
can't help notice that the people breathe quite differently
in the swirl of les événements
as if they've let their lungs relax
    after lifetimes holding breath.
Also the looks are different, Arnaud's aware of that,
that is the ones who eat his wares
now watch and see from time to time
whereas before he was not seen
while with the people on the street
a smiling knowing plays inside the eyes,
a we-don't-have-to-talk-about-it shine
and Arnaud puzzles on this when he *thinks* at all.
    And now to do the pears.

But a certain Abbé, not the one who takes the bakings of Arnaud,
studies, calculates,
has reduced the language to a knife
to slice away the dead skin covering that holds inside a brilliant fly.
  He says about this brilliant fly:
What is the third estate: why, everything
What has it been till now: nothing
What does it ask: to be something.

  And there
shall wither from the body (or be sliced) the extra things,
the useless things,
no bogging down in sentiments about the organism's history,
who cares if Zeus's blood bubbled through a tail?
No appendix of the past will hinder flight,
  and this new creature she will go
even if at first or other times
not all her legs and wings incline the same.
Push at least in concert to shove off the skin
and rise into the sun-splashed air,
breathe deep, breathe fresh...

and jump, and jump, for we have opened on a restless day
and it is hard to stay in place.

     *   *   *

An Archæology of Revolution

Now another leap to find some common threads, how's this:
the Prussian generals will let the goateed man come through,
pass through,
since he might ease their burden, let them turn their cannon west,
to boot add grain fields farther than the raven flies
and though in shameless company a man will be pilloried for this,
this is not his error, not his sin —
      the butchers aren't owed anything.
The ground steeps, the bodies reach the stage of pemmican,
      the boys who've never wet their touch to turn a page
run howling into fire-storms,
no the butchers aren't owed anything.
      And the train will roll across the ancient plain
into the freest country in the world where
Peace and Bread and Land will win the day —
how could they not?
Though hearts weighed down by Russian gods
will groan when prices get a name
and some will moan it is too much, too dear...
but that is not the error, not his sin.
      And in the deathkicks of the Second Estate
a family of symbols in a basement they will fall,
and girls and boys you can call them innocent
but as it's written, woe to women who are with child
and women who are nursing in those days,
      and no one will moan for them
and at that time there will be great affliction,
and none among the hypocrites will moan the lesser ones

and that is not his error, that is not his sin.
The sin will come when the man who rode across the plain to slay
> the beast,
to bring the temple down, will think to raise another one anew,
will not know that one chain smashed another can be forged,
especially if chains are in demand.

Thus with that other writer of the tracts — the abbé of the penly knife,
> the one from '89 —
he's straightening roads for Georgian Bonapartes.
And yes the sin is similar, objectively it might be said, though
the abbé was triumvir in a coup at last,
knew what he did and took a chateau as his recompense
while the Russian died with just his suit,
taking bread and tea, no more.
But integrity can't save the sin, objectively that is.

While the monster and the temple turn into machine,
> grind on,
>> grind on.

*   *   *

An Archæology of Revolution

    Now, the army everywhere
is birthing bored, frustrated sorts;
in the towns of hot Castile   (1936)
where Generals under uniforms still wear the rotting skins
plots are in play,
        dreams to cancel all the errors that have grown.
And they are errors, no?
"Weren't we right to rise?"

                (The King he didn't have the nerve
                listened when the masses hollered
                should have waxed his ears all tight
                with the fat from hatters boiled)

        There's young Montse on the coast shouting that equality
            should reign
and that the glorious Spanish state be disappeared
into the shifting bumping comités of common women and their men,
and what's she doing, hija de puta,
standing by the holy door
while orange Levant breezes kiss her skin,
holding up that can of petrol, trying to decide —
        are sacred buildings worth some blood or not?
        Cut her throat before they'd bother ask her why.

(The King he didn't have the nerve
listened when the masses hollered
should have waxed his ears all tight
with the fat from hatters boiled)

Counterpoint.
Should dens of evil get the torch or not?
This church: house of obscurantism, superstition,
throws the dead priests' stinking rags over the light, over the light.
On the other hand the stone is fine,
is made by men,
perhaps it could just witness to the dialectic of the sickest sort —
the glory of the minds and hands of flesh brought spirit,
but *their* working spirit, into rock and wood,
inspired all the while in grovelling of the soul.
And we'll just build no more.

Pero por otro lado, la oportunidad de demostrar victoria,
la conquista por la libertad!
"I'll throw my cleansing fire water now, abomination of the privileged,
and bring you down,
scorch you clean,
but... but...
we need each drop
to run the things that waste them at the front."

An Archaeology of Revolution

Oh Montse's tangled in her spot.
      The Generals will cut her head off anyway.

           (The King he didn't have the nerve
           listened when the masses hollered
           should have waxed his ears all tight
           with the fat from hatters boiled)

Meanwhile, hey, do you see him,
he's in that sharp brown suit sitting at the bar
a de Kuyper son many times removed
      (if that clan's recalled)
though not a drop of Dutch blood dribbles through his veins.
He elbow rests in the fading light beside the glass
and thinks about his line of work,
      maybe the woman in his house,
a second for his boyhood window on the port at Marsa Matruh,
a birthday party in the Athens house,
then back to work, the mortar shipment just arranged:
papers signed in Paris, weapons built not far from Prague,
a train then a boat to Valencia.
Though nothing, nothing compared to the deal
      pulled off the month before,
a deal resounding in divinity,
reminiscent of the Christ extending loaves and fish…
      that's it, the loaves and fish.
For what he did that time can be grasped no other way
but by the sacred reference,

defying laws of any natural sort:

acquired through a contact from a Belgian firm

five shipments of the latest anti-aircraft gun, then

sold them, contract's here somewhere,

to the Ministry of Defence (Madrid) and four days later —

here's the part divine — again, again, with a Hamburg partner

to the ROWAK,

who moved it to the HISMA

whose job it is to get it to the Franco boys.

Like that, the loaves and fishes.

Guns for one, rent by modern magic into two.

Though like the seaside lunch,
      without conclusive evidence that everyone was fed.

          (The King he didn't have the nerve
          listened when the masses hollered
          should have waxed his ears all tight
          with the fat from hatters boiled)

Then back to Montse and the weighing of the times,

the jug of petrol jiggling beside. Should she strike the match?

And the prophets — M. Bakunin and another more reputable —
      will chat with her:

An Archæology of Revolution

"So is it necessary to remind you sirs,
to what point the religious influences demoralize
and corrupt the peoples?"

"And he healed many who were ill with various diseases...
And all ate, and were fed..."

"...founded in blood, historically baptized in blood..."

"He woke and scolded the wind and said to the sea: silence, be still.
And the sea subsided and there was great calm."

"How hard it will be for those with
money to enter the Kingdom of God...
And the masses heard him with great pleasure..."

"...And nothing that hasn't been analyzed and
confirmed by experience or by the most severe
critique can be accepted by it..."

"Turn away from the scribes
who desire the salutations in the public places
and the foremost couches at the dinners,
who eat up the houses of the widows,
and pray long as an excuse..."

"One solitary lord in the sky
makes thousands on the earth."

"For they feared him,

for all the populace was smitten by his teaching."

"Naked and null as nothing;...

filling and enriching himself

with all the realities of the world."

"The kings of the Gentiles are as lords over them,

and those who exercise authority are called

their benefactors. Not so you..."

"...prohibited for no other reason

than that it was the will of God.

And if our first parents had obeyed, all

the human race would have remained in a state

of the most humiliating slavery. Their rebellion freed us

(mythically speaking, of course)."

"...But woe to you who are rich,

for you have had all your consolation.

And do you think I came to give peace on earth?

I came to cast fire on the fire."

And then, decided: through our good daughter Montse His will was done.

The cleansing tongues would light the way ahead.

IX

Didn't like politics. For him fast cars...

While another was the motion man
was Nick,
at first in one way, later in a stationary way
already moving as a womb-bound lump
when the Earth quit Alexandria.
Rhythms set out on the deck,
white foam pushing hard away that door of Africa,
Greekness pulled to scatter still.
Sshhh! the circles of the blade played a dark brine song,
we know this tune, the dark brine song!
Movement sown into a sprouting brain
if not to manifest traditionally.

    And some, of Nick, made dire forecasts
made them of the movement planted deep inside,

..wushshshshsssh...

When later family had settled down
saw strangeness in the way young Nick inside his eyes
held basketballs, their launch
      the instant hung in air
when all the future, past, stretched low in rushing rides
and they did not know he strove to stretch the instant,

make of it a bridge,
        secure the motion in the middle of itself;
all they thought was here's a boy who stares at globes.

But Nick he sorted through all movement's ways and shapes,
tracked its progress through the sea and air
and on the ground,
        registered the words and notes the pistons sang
squeezed by burning juices of the earth
in the garage where the uncles worked;
could play them to himself in bed
could show them to himself in sleep

...zzzhzzzhzz...

        So from a white book
watched the leaps post-Icarus
reaching back behind the turbofan
that sucks in freezing breaths above
and mixes them with burning juice
(the lavad earth propelled some finished shapes so distant from itself).
Nicky followed this, trailed it back,
then snuck out on a tarmac aged eleven
saw the blazing air scorch cool and push a Boeing liquid blue —
then for his trouble took three whacks,
        Nick's parents were like that.

And the march of shapes that hauled and sped through history,
Nicky's history
> (contextualizer he was not):
Leonardo's bats that never left their mothers' teats;
hydrogen bellies (set for flaming death);
Ader's vapour owl that just got off the ground then down;
the Wright boys' forty metres shadowing the field.
And a picture he had of Louis Blériot
taken on what looks to be a gentle slope,
> the bulky man in flying gear just left the plane,
police and suits to greet him at the Channel cross: (1909)

A squares-coat man, his back to us, another, Blériot,
triangle of a chat
(the grass cut short) —
this shot young Nicky tacked up by his bed.
Right beside a Hawker Hart, metal light,
where wind whipped 'round a pilot's head
that taking turns itself became the wind,
and a giant pontooned bird,
dragon eyes and a beak that twirled its blades,
a mammoth killer-insect springing at the guests —
all these he kept.
> And Nick had dreams of being in the kitchen of it all,
Concorde's gut
where the deafening roar is made
where hot gases blast
and no sweet winds even dull the noise

nor strap down devils of men's brains.

    These devils have their way
and howl, they bellow high and
hurtle over seas as fast as they might want
because, at last, they can.

    So in the kitchen where this roar is made
Nicky would have liked to cook
but he did not, he did not,
came to tend the uncles' hearth instead
where lesser speeds were made;
drove a TransAm like so many sons of Attica
paid no rent before the wedding day
watched the baseball on the screen,
sometimes in the station eyed the rail-snakes winding in...

Knew the movements all
but took few contexts in his head.
Well not true, not quite;
    one he had were flanks of Dundas Street
run straight east when cars day-rolled,
vision held while corners of his eyes
took in the grounds of tree and flat,
houses coloured rosely brown and grey.
Plus the progress of the movement, its story through the times,
this was all the context Nicky had,
    no more.

An Archaeology of Revolution

He was a focussed man, a man upon a track.
    In his twenties late just a watcher he was not yet —
Nick played ball still with the lads from school
in the summer took a shark fin on a board
to cut the lake's blue glass,
ran a half a marathon for kids with blood disease,
could chase women in a bar
but the dampening was on its way;
he stayed in place little by little more and more, perceptibly,
got married, had a child,
never let up on the beer and lamb and marinated pork,
began on weekends sending thin roots down into the couch.
Perceptibly.
And could in any case
unhinge the jagged teeth of gears
or check a valve refused to close resting on his knees,
    or lying on his back.

    At forty-two he would be tough to recognize
by those who'd watched him as a youth,
thickened by denial of his soul:
puff of face, middle wide, sometimes seen to tired droop
when he thought no one was around.
But he'd still joke with friends of thirty years
encountered on the street
in the same sprung voice
    light like leaping air.
Light as ten-year-olds in a field of grain.

Later, all this done, settled for a while,
he watched the water calm and wet one day
then read about a basket woven tight that Ganges drifts.
No sound to imitate, you'd think, but there is some,
    there's one

...whhhwhhh...

Portuguese green boomerang plying fishing shoals
placed against the rec. room wall —
Nick was coming back.
Set up by his window model of a giant Maori craft
hooked for war and death,
dragons sliding jagged lines
screaming silently for heads,
sharp-hoofed for war and death —
Nick was coming back.
Bought a quarter junk for the basement
    (still that's very big)
displacing basket of a dog,
dwarfing leaves and stems
all types.
    To sail green waters of a rug, with
    sails like chunks of canvas torn instead of cut
    slanting still toward the filmy sky and
painted orange-red, the birds and dragons at the back,
floral serpents, cool and burning colours there;

An Archæology of Revolution

could be a cotton mat was rolled on top the deck
so one upon the restless gleaming back could sleep,
yet never absolutely stop.

    Like that was Nick,
though sometimes seen to pause and droop.

X

The thing
> of course
>> is that you're here

no other realm
> and when
>> is now

for him for them for you.
> Try to stretch the molecules
>> push against the walls

of the almost yielding place
> but waking
>> find them flawlessly

(even on a day of falling moons
> or strolls across a carpet fat of leaves)
>> boxing the dimensions of the skull.

An Archaeology of Revolution

VII (*still more*)

And he was called Deng (that's 'dung' in English to you and me)
and was author of many great sayings, this one not the least:
    'To get rich is glorious!'
    A sloganeer if ever there was one.
And he said China had to open to the marketplace,
there would be no keeping out the power-ranger factories;
    the people would be taught to grab,
but the state would hold the heights and the Party —
steady, ever steady — keep the helm.
Thus socialism's built.

And the blue elephant inside my closet
eats spaghetti morning noon and night except for Wednesdays
    when he has his grass.

While more or less at the same time — after the scandal of the tapes —
a man rose up who despised the state
and captured the imaginations everywhere.
He floated from a land called California
and said that he despised the state but armed it past its nose
and spent more public green than anyone before —
    can you imagine that?
and we wondered quite a bit (speaking for the committee here)
until we learned much later on he had this malady
that eats away the brain (the one my Nana suffered from
till she didn't know the son she'd borne).

      And there are tales —
they remain unproven but we're satisfied —
of an inheritor of the machine already dead, embalmed,
but on the freezing days propped up to watch the workers
marching past, or the missiles as the case might be
who in a tally carefully recorded by a double agent
(who remains concealed even today)
was found to have contributed, in meetings of the cabinet,
      and even in his corpsy state,
to two, that's 2, decisions more than Mr. California
as he sat in on his.
One day we will reveal this agent's name and how he got the goods.

      So on they go, the salesman types
who struggled with eleventh grade but landed in some Ministry,
the drunk who roars and bellies in the old red walls,
the Vice-President (Groundbird, by name)
who re-reads Plato every year
but thinks they chat in Latin in the Salvador
("de verdad, si tuviéramos una educación así,
pero faltan sillas, pupitres además");
this craft can only be perfected by the few,
      that's sure.

An Archæology of Revolution

    And among other extraordinary things
tumbling in the epoch necessarily would count
(you might not think this fits, but wait)
a certain baseball game upon a crappy rug
when everyone just creamed the hide until the score was 24-10
and fielders, catchers pitched
and a clerk among the forty-somethings thought he could go down
upon the turf and take a bat and whack it far enough.

    But there it is, now isn't it, the nutshell thing:
that finding the soft alley could be a Willy Loman act,
even if ironically in this field it's well out of reach
    (but here is where the refried dreams are spent).
Yet more irony than that, still more: put down the dusty wood and
look, look up! The bimbos play the universal game!

    *   *   *

And he was a young man still, the Portuguese Otelo,
bold, decided
    (hair all there, if grey across cut short),
surged determined from a cauldron
burst carnation air
when the lid at last came off.   (1974)
There in a place westerly where the earth once rocked,
broke men's old foundations
and a river took itself into the lashing sea

and the city spread up hills as if to thrust in the gods' home —
there, Otelo too would have re-built, in another way.

You see his strong, shaved face,
        his lips are set to speak upon a truth, a truth,
no wipe of fertilizer spread to cultivate career;
at certain moments things lay clear,
the possibilities are bared, the smirking falls away.
At forty he is sure:
In a world beyond the platitudes it will be done today
        or tried again at least,
the old mistakes will see no repetition.
Intermediaries swept away, the 'genius few' dispersed,
the city to its place, so when in future people get it wrong
it really will be their own fault.

At sixty he is proud and sharp, Otelo,
harried by the beast he'd slay,
repeating calmly that the shifting, bumping
gatherings of flesh and brain
        of women and their men
still loom for us,
for he knows the ways and roads wind long, so long;
most men and women lose themselves,
think Thursday's bend's a world.
Not he.

                *   *   *

An Archæology of Revolution

Now,
what joined Otelo bursting with the lid into carnation air?
    What lingers in its wake?
Too much too long to be exhaustive
and many things are repetitions,
    the heart can sigh creatively but once, or twice.
A burst of colour on the walls, and every town and city,
village named its street, the number 25,
and says a sniffing writer in a snooty travel magazine
the Ritz perched over Parque Eduardo VII
struggled when the ones who washed the sheets bit bigger themes
    (Big glorious f....n' deal, we say to that).
And a thick black robe too hot for summer's night was pulled away,
all open flung the doors
(though the women have to run to Spain
when something goes awry)
and Africa reversed the flow,
emptied souls and bodies in the Praça do Comercio.
Alas as everywhere, the spirits and the dreams were cooled
to embers ruffled by a breath.
Though some, Otelo's one, know Thursday's bend is not a world.
We'll see, we'll see.

And last year Larry came, and said the soup was good,
    quite thick and good,
and that the tile work all around his head was fine
and that you tire walking everywhere, up down Lisboa's hills.
We'll see, we'll see.

An Archaeology of Revolution

XI

Now gentlemen, I'm gettin' just a little tired
of yer high falutin techno-crap.

Some scrawny worshippers,
bone-armed dripethas with sweaters too tight
and skin the shade of milk sat too long for the cat
will tell us (as they bend toward the huaca of the plastic glass)
that oh! the world's 'within';
hurry, hunch, peer and gaze, strike the rodent's back,
get that head inclined,
forget the tree that gives its life,
    forget the dusty ground and snowy slope
when new dimensions, 010001-land opens up,
then with all creation at the fingertips run free!
Learn German less Frau Rominger
    yourself! yourself! Wired up
vote on the budget Wednesday next right from the terminal
then write a piece of the eternal novel floating out in space;
with shifting middles, ends and starts it makes us
weekend makers of the age!
For all I know fucking can be virtual,
which for the dripethas at least might constitute advance.
Even wear a tattoo of the circuits bleeding under passé skin,
oh yearn to shed our human flesh.
But a break, please, oh a break oh Harry Dinkmuscle!

Nor neutrality will we give.
Too much has already run under the bridge.
The precursors after all left their deadening mark
on asses everywhere
and yapping heads
made the generations fat before their time.
Don't sing me that song Mr. Smooth about it being *just* a means,
just just to be used either well or badly, badly or well
because even if there's truth in that
tis a sedative on lips like yours,
a calm-down-the-lunatic tune to croon to the likes of me
but your flame's no hotter than a puddle on the street
and what you go along with could rot us in its stink.

The revolution of the digits,
that's the one that lets us with a flick
watch eighty channels in a night —
you'll chuckle, show you think it's dumb
then buy the girlfriend's watch on the shopping show
and anger when the talk grows serious,
      growl "the essence stays the same,
the tools are new, but the essence stays the same."
You'll see no need to watch the things, be vigilant.

For they, or it, do carry drives and wants, their own,
breed like rat or bird,
know as well as any that to species be is the motive of us all
and like the lions under Kiliman and wolves up north

make others in the neighbourhood bend to their ways.

But have a god they do (even as great temples to themselves are built) who may one day clear his head, get off his knees,

    enforce a decent bondage...

So gentlemen put down yer crap.

XII

1.

> While in the summer of '90-something,
> as a manner to conclude,
> there was stone furniture,
> > the tables wearing checkers on their backs,

hickories and poplars all alone
just like the marigolds.
> Alexander Douglas (that's the neighbour, right?)

by the day before to drop himself upon a bench;
he noticed this park doesn't lack a garden wall.
> Two strips of carpet lawn stretch broad and thick

and precisely now (I am so rarely up at five)
the air is creamy, making promises of baths of heat to come,
while visible up at the picture's top are white sea birds
who drift across the rising sky
> as threads of ruffled earth strung thinly out.

(Not much love is spent on them down here,
but they were born in risk and paid as many dues as us).
A squirrel shoots down its trunk.

2.

Gums where teeth once were,
raining tangled hair and skinny as a well-fed female Bergen-Belsenite
    is one.
    Another is an orange mop,
another grey and black-maned man whose eyes,
the colour of Ontario's turned earth,
earth moistened in the lowlands of an ocean's arm,
would elsewhere argue with his booze-rouge nose.
Another is a younger one whose legs spring out from this land too;
    they're up, these four,
    the threads of earth have passed.
The task: line up the cash to swing a bottle
from the wines and spirits store just down the street.

    "And I'm not sleeping in that shit-box place again;
I lost my pen and cigarettes last night,
had them in my jacket pocket, jacket I was wearing when I slept."
It's just they don't serve eggs and bacon, cereal,
in many city parks.

3.

Checkers next with the morning gentlemen,
skins sun-dried through a life of putting down the roads,
    cutting pampered grass,
feeling morning winds slash as the garbage goes into the bag.
He scoops the plastic sack of pieces out a pocket
that's so deep it reaches near the knee,
    places them carefully.
Your friend Alphonse will take the blacks,
and Gord the red
    Alphonse will take the blacks
    and Gord the red.

On this spot right here,
where pieces move under old men's digits thick
    some others fell one time
light-armed, exhausted,
trying hard to catch their breath after running from a battlefield;
also a red man once was killed.
    And here today
just metres 'cross the pavement sitting on a bench
two other types negotiate the selling of a company,
    a helmet company
and the sun grows hot
and water's sprinkled in the shade
and E. Henderson who likes to watch for teenage boys
    is finishing his plastic cup of tea.

4.

And there, before the offices disgorge their lunching folk
        Haydar Kocgiri sits to wait
to talk about the film he made on Turkey's killings in the Kurdistan,
to show his tortured wrists burned pink then brown;
with all this *you* and I,
and the heat lights orange tints upon your hair
and draws three beads of sweat
and paints the gleam I like so much and here,
not there,
here not there to say again
retroactively withdraws the doubt, misgivings that I've ever had
(or worse have said or acted out)
about longevity, our endlessness,
entwining that will never come undone.
        Now there are four beads upon your face,
the helmet company's been sold,
one of the Indians is getting up to beg.

2.

Seven bucks, more than one needs,
it's down the street abreast (the red-haired Anglo-Saxon stays),
back in minutes with a litre bottle of the cheap
Niagara something '92
and again the red-mop he declines —
better on the street to stay alert, he thinks,
but on the sprawl of grass the others drink so deep,
roll out some blankets from a pack to rest.
    Eyes the colour of Ontario's turned earth
it is a day of wicked, wicked heat.
    The nearly toothless woman knew a man,
a Micmac Newfoundman who when he'd had a half-a-Seagram's
would buy some moose from Indian friends
—veal if there was none—
and make a stew with carrots by the load.
Shit, she'd like some now,
    even if there's wicked wicked heat.

4.

There we listen to Kocgiri, *you* and I,
watch a stained and shabby guy
who's replaced the helmet company
count a giant pile of roses we suppose he's meant to sell.
Kocgiri was in prison, a Turkish one at that
       they burned his wrists cruel pink then brown
the marigolds soak up the sun —
       we think it's time to eat.
And the checkers men look like they're finishing,
pop the disks back in that sack and then
into the pocket that would almost brush a knee.
       I think about entwining (here not there)
that never can undo, a filling of infinity —
       you also think it's time to eat.
And the man is troubled by the counting of the roses,
roses red as life gushed in the air;
he's always stopping, starting over.
We'll wait until he finishes his inventory.

Like its cooking sun the afternoon drifts down,
faces trading, bodies lounging in the grass under the trees
       then up;
a trace of cool appears with dusk.
The man with flowers tries to sell.

An Archæology of Revolution

5.

    A priest who hid his collar well (by leaving it to wash)
       sinks his face into his hands by way of following the sun.
Oh God it spreads until it fills you up, he thinks,
and tries inside his head to see something again,
       to cast another kind of light but there is none for him.

And when the night gets on
there are moans beneath a tree,
a woman bent over a man
and they don't care *too much* if they are seen
(what would the Bishop Strachan say?)
       gasping pushing moaning
not as loud as they want but
    louder than they think,
gurgles from two bodies' springs
       no rivers anywhere in sight
while Andre
(the younger one of eyes just like Ontario's turned earth)
stays put, will spurn that fleaful box of men.
       After he listens to the sex
and feels some money found,
two dollars from a bathroom floor,
off he drifts to sleep to dream
of hotdogs, corn roasted to a dusky hue,

sandwiches stretching out the mandibles

(unlike his stomach of the day

the one of dreams is not yet shrunk into a pickled knot).

But there are no strangers' kitchens rousing him tonight

    nor dinner boys delivering bags

but sounds,

    a sound of pain that never even follows bucketfuls of wine,

a nasty gesture dishing up a final sense (of what?);

it booms with every beat,

he falls down from his knees

and Andre hears a clapping on the earth.

    His head bows to the green,

his nose sensing that he needs rest.

The air is not so warm as in the day,

    no light tints orange in the hair.

END STEP TWO.

An Archæology of Revolution

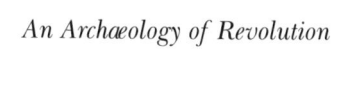

Historical Glossary

Bakker, Jim
U.S. Assemblies of God televangelist sentenced to 45 years in prison for fraud and tax irregularities. Also touched by sex scandal in 1987. Released after serving fraction of sentence. Wife Tammy Faye left her husband while he was in prison.

Ball, John
Cornish clergyman who advocated a classless society in 14th-century England and a leading figure in the 1381 peasant rebellion. With its defeat, Ball was executed.

Child, Julia
Twentieth-century US cookbook author, television personality and promoter of French cuisine.

Gracchus, Tiberius and Gaius
Second-century BC Roman politicians (and brothers) who favoured the distribution of public lands, used and controlled by the rich, among the landless.

HISMA (Compañía Hispano Maroquí de Transportes) and ROWAK (Rohstoffe-und-Waren-Einkaufsgesellschaft)
Firms set up in 1936 for the purpose of exchanging German aid and Spanish raw material payments between Berlin and the Nationalist forces.

Lippi, Fra Filippo

Florentine painter, 1406-1469. Important works include "The Annunciation" and the altarpiece "Coronation of the Virgin." In Lippi's workshop was apprenticed a young man by the name of **Sandro Botticelli**.

Mackenzie, William Lyon

Journalist, politician, leader of the 1837 Upper Canada rebellion against the local elite and British rule. The war's sole battle resulted in a convincing victory for the British forces.

Necker, Jacques

Swiss banker and Louis XVI's Director General of Finance.

Pompey, or **Gnaeus Pompeius Magnus**

Roman General of late Republic who defeated the 'Marian' faction in Sicily and Africa in the early 80s BC and later, with considerable difficulty, put down Sertorius' rising in Spain. Subsequently returned to Italy to make a token contribution to the final defeat of the slave army led by **Spartacus**. From 61 to 54 triumvir before unsuccessfully clashing with Julius Caesar for control of the state. Killed in Egypt in 48.

Primo de Rivera, José Antonio

Leader of the Falange, Spain's fascist movement. Executed in prison by the Republican government during the Civil War, 1936-39.

Saraiva de Carvalho, Otelo
Leading figure in Portugal's Carnation Revolution of 1974. Spent five years in jail in the 1980s, accused of organizing political assassinations carried out by the armed group FP-25. Otelo denies he authored or supported any terrorist activities. He continues to defend a model of politics based on direct democracy through citizens' assemblies.

Scipio Aemilianus, or Africanus the Younger
An admirer of Hellenistic culture and leading Roman personality better known for two military accomplishments: the destruction of Carthage in 146 BC and the capture of the Iberian town of Numantia (near present-day Soria) after a lengthy siege and ferocious resistance in 133. This settlement had been a focal point of Celtiberian struggle against Roman rule in 'Spain'.

Sertorius, Quintus
Roman politician, officer who, with considerable local backing, led the 'Spanish' breakaway from Rome beginning in 82 BC. Died with rebellion's collapse in 72. But Rome's problems weren't finished; the slave revolt led by Spartacus was already underway.

Sieyes, Emmanuel or the Abbé Sieyes
A key thinker and ideologist of the French revolution, author of, among other works, *What is the Third Estate?* This book articulated the aspirations of the French middle classes on the question of how they should be represented in the Assembly. If the clergy, nobility and the commons were to meet and vote separately, as they had when the Estates of the Nation had last been called by the King in 1614, the

people would most likely be unable to carry through legislative change. But with members of the three estates counted together, the representatives of the commons would easily outnumber the two more conservative groups. Sieyes's formula: "What is the Third Estate? Everything", was perhaps as earth-rocking a slogan, in its day, as "Peace, Bread and Land" 128 years later.

Sulla, Lucius Cornelius

Officer in Italian Social War (90-88 BC) and later victor in Roman Civil War, ended 82. Dictator until 79. Died the following year near Naples.

Tahuantinsuyu

"Land of the four quarters," that territory along the west coast of South America under the sway of the Incan empire in the fifteenth and early sixteenth centuries. Its inhabitants were ravaged by European-introduced plague before a single white face appeared in the region.

Erratum in glossary. Entry should read:

Ball, John
Excommunicated clergyman who advocated...

Quotations in VII are from Richmond Lattimore's translation of the *Four Gospels and the Revelation*, published by Farrar, Strauss, Giroux (New York, 1979), and M. Bakunin's *Obras, Vol. 3*, published by Ediciones Júcar (Madrid, 1977).
Passages from the latter work were translated by the author.

An Archaeology of Revolution is Marc Young's first book of poetry.